Introductic

**AHNE Bryniau Clwyd
Clwydian Range AONB**

CU00685577

The **Clwydian Range**, designate
Natural Beauty, is a chain o
between the Vale of Clwyd an
in North Wales, covering an a
Range extends south for 22 miles from Prestatyn and the
coast to Nant y Garth pass, with Moel Famau in the centre, its highest point at
1,820ft. Within the AONB, and managed by Denbighshire Countryside Service,
are Loggerheads and Moel Famau Country Parks – the latter, with its impressive upland landscape, being one of the largest in Wales.

The Clwydian Range offers a diversity of high quality landscape scenery,
including heather moorland, open green hills, limestone crags, woodland,
river valleys, and rolling farmland. It also contains many important historical
and archaelogical sites from pre-historic times to the more recent industrial
age. Most notable are the six impressive Iron-Age hill forts, one of the highest
concentrations in Western Europe.

It is a wonderful walking area, offering panoramic views. Running through
the full length of the Range, linking most of the hills, is one of the most scenic
sections of Offa's Dyke Path National Trail.

This new fully revised and extended edition of my original book explores
its diverse scenery and rich heritage through twenty-two linked circular walks,
incorporating the Offa's Dyke Path from Prestatyn hillside to Llandegla. The
routes, which range from 4 – 7 miles, follow public rights of way or permissive
paths, and visit new designated Open Access land that became available to the
public in 2005. The routes are within the capability of most people and many
contain shorter walk options. *A key feature is that individual walks can easily
be linked, in various combinations, to provide longer and more challenging
day walks if required.* Walking boots are recommended, along with appropri-
ate clothing to protect against the elements. Please remember that the condi-
tion of paths/bridleways can vary according to season and weather. Contact
the relevant local Highways Department or Countryside Service regarding any
problems encountered (see page 40 for details).

Each walk has a detailed map and description which enables the route
to be followed without difficulty, but be aware that changes in detail can
occur at any time (e.g. new stile/field boundary). The location of each walk is
shown on the back cover and a summary of the key characteristics of each is
also given. This includes an estimated walking time, but allow more time to
enjoy the scenery. Most walks are accessible by bus. For further details of the
extensive Vale Rider network and Clwydian Ranger summer service telephone
01824 706968.

Please observe the country code and take particular care not to damage
any ancient site visited.

Enjoy your walking!

Walk I
GRAIG FAWR & COED YR ESGOB

DESCRIPTION This 4 mile walk (**A**) provides a fascinating exploration of the low limestone hills at the northern end of the Clwydian Range, once mined for lead and zinc, and quarried for stone. It takes you to the top of Graig Fawr, owned by the National Trust and across Prestatyn hillside on the Offa's Dyke Path, both offering extensive views. After passing through Coed yr Esgob, an area of ancient oak woodland, it returns along the former Dyserth to Prestatyn railway line – now a popular recreational walkway. Allow about 2½ hours. A shorter 3 mile walk (**B**) is included.

START Dyserth to Prestatyn Walkway car park on the outskirts of Dyserth. SJ 062793.

DIRECTIONS The car park adjoins the A5151 where the road dips on the eastern side of Dyserth.

I Return to the main road and follow it LEFT past the Anglia complex and up the hill past houses. Just beyond the speed road sign, turn LEFT then go along the right of two tracks ahead, to cross a stile alongside The Glen. Follow a rough track (can be muddy) to its end at a facing gate. Here turn RIGHT and follow the long field boundary on the left up to a stile. Go across the next field to reach a road, which you follow LEFT to a T-junction. Go to the National Trust car park and entrance to Graig Fawr. *Graig Fawr is a notable limestone hill and a Site of Special Scientific Interest. It is managed by the National Trust as an important area for nature conservation and a local amenity.*

2 Just beyond the kissing-gate, bear LEFT to follow a path, which shortly bends and rises up the lower gorse-covered slope to eventually reach the summit trig point for panoramic views along the North Wales coast and to the mountains of Snowdonia. *Of nearer interest, looking down to the SW, is the ruin of the Clive Engine House. It was built in the 1860s to house a massive steam engine for pumping water from the Talargoch lead and zinc mines. The main shaft was 1000' deep, but the high cost of keeping the mine dry led to its closure in 1884. From the trig point head SE. over nearby limestone ridges, then follow the clear path down and across the undulating terrain towards a large wall.* (For **Walk B**, at a telegraph pole just before a waymarker post, do a sharp U-turn to follow the waymarked Dyserth circular walk past sheepfolds. It heads towards the coast then

descends steeply through the trees. At the bottom, turn left and follow the path down the wood edge to go through a kissing gate onto the Dyserth-Prestatyn Way, near the Meliden good shed site. Follow it left back to the start.) For the main walk continue to a kissing gate in the wall, then follow the road LEFT.

3 At a junction by Laburnum Cottage (*one of several cottages built by miners on common land*) turn LEFT then RIGHT on Offa's Dyke Path. The path takes you down a drive, and passes the side of Red Roofs, then soon crosses the open gorse-clad hillside with fine views. The path then descends to a kissing-gate. Follow the Offa's Dyke Path through the trees, past two side paths to re-emerge on the open hillside. Continue alongside a fence above a disused quarry and across the hillside. *Large quantities of limestone has been extracted from local quarries over centuries, primarily to produce lime for the chemical industry, for use in steel making, and as a fertilizer.*

4 At a waymarked path junction leave the Offa's Dyke Path to follow the path signposted Coed yr Esgob (Bishop's Wood) – *an area of unspoilt natural predominantly oak woodland, which is designated as a Site of Special Scientific Interest, and provides a rich haven for plants, animals and birds.* The path steadily descends through the wood and past the entrance to the Fish Mine. *This calcite and lead mine, which closed at the beginning of the 20thC, was allegedly named* because its spoil tip resembled the shape of a fish. Another possible explanation might be the presence of fossilised fish in the limestone. At the bottom of the wood, by a waymarker post, turn LEFT and follow a path along the wood edge. Soon after a kissing gate, you reach a lane. Go through the kissing gate on your right and down the field to join the Prestatyn-Dyserth Way.

5 Follow it LEFT. *The former Prestatyn – Dyserth branch railway, which linked to the main Chester-Holyhead line, was opened in 1869 to serve the local mines and quarries. A passenger service ran between 1905 – 1930, at its peak operating 16 trains a day. The line was eventually closed in 1973. The old line passes an information board at the site of Meliden Goods Shed, then continues beneath Graig Fawr, through attractive woodland, under two bridges and across the river back to the start. En route you pass a hill on which is the site of Dyserth Castle built by Henry 111 in 1241 and destroyed in 1263 by Llewelyn ap Gruffydd, the last of the native Welsh princes. Few remains now survive.*

*B*efore leaving the area, a visit to Dyserth waterfall and the Church of St. Bridget and St. Cwyfan with its fine medieval stained glass window is highly recommended.

Walk 2
MARION FRITH & MOEL HIRADDUG

DESCRIPTION A delightful 5 mile walk across undulating countryside, featuring two old watermills, the small limestone hill of Marion Ffrith, and a 16thC inn in Cwm. There is also an option to visit for the first time the delightful limestone hill of Moel Hiraddug, the most northerly of the Clwydian Iron-Age hillforts, now a designated Open Access area. Moel Hiraddug, sadly scarred by quarrying for limestone, offers extensive views. In the 19thC, part of a 2nd century BC. ceremonial shield was found here. Allow about 3 hours.

START Dyserth to Prestatyn Walkway car park. SJ 062793. See **Walk I**.

1 Follow the main road LEFT past the Anglia complex. After about 120 yards take a signposted path on the opposite side below water treatment works. Follow the waymarked stiled path along the course of an old railway line to a minor road. *In 1884, H.D. Pochin, a local landowner, at his own expense built, the first ¾ mile of a proposed extension of the Prestatyn-Dyserth railway to the nearby village of Trelawynd. It was never completed beyond Marion Mill.* Follow the road LEFT past the remains of Grove Mill. On the bend take the Offa's Dyke Path (Marion Cwm) along the stone track ahead to Marion Mill. *The fast flowing stream once turned the waterwheels of several mills for generating power for turning corn into flour and for the fulling process in the preparation of yarns and woven fabric.*

2 Here turn RIGHT and follow the stiled OD. Path along an enclosed green track, then the edge of two fields to a road. Follow it along a nearby green track, over a stile on the left, then through two fields to reach a track. Follow it LEFT past a farm to cross a stile on the right. The OD. Path heads up to a stile, then rises steadily across the open pasture of Marian Ffrith guided by waymarker posts and down to the road at the hamlet of Marian Cwm. Follow the OD. Path over a nearby stile, and two further ones, then up a large field to a stile near the left-hand corner onto a road. Cross the stile opposite, then follow the long field edge up to another road. Turn LEFT.

3 After 25 yards, leave the OD. Path by taking a signposted path on your right up a green track by a wood. On the bend, ignore a stile, but turn RIGHT alongside the fence to a nearby stile, then on to another one. Briefly go along a track, then follow the fence on your left to a stile above a stone building. Continue near an old boundary to a stile, then follow the path down through mixed woodland, turning RIGHT at a waymarker post down to a road. Keep ahead, then turn LEFT down another road into Cwm. Go past the Blue Lion Inn, then take a path signposted to Dyserth on the right. Go up the field to a stile by a wood. The path now angles up to another stile, climbs the initially steep field to a stile, then descends the next field edge to a road.

4 Go through a kissing gate opposite. (To visit Moel Hiraddug: About 25 yards beyond the kissing gate, head RIGHT up the slope between areas of gorse to join a higher distinct path which passes through an area of small trees/shrubs to emerge near a gate in a wall. Bear left and head up the left-hand edge of Moel Hiraddug, passing to the left of a transmitter mast to reach its highest point. Walk along its limestone ridge towards the sea. At a fence overlooking the old quarry, bear right, then follow a path back across the eastern slope. After passing beneath the mast, bear right to rejoin and descend your outward route.) The main path now goes along the base of Moel Hiraddug, soon descending through woodland.

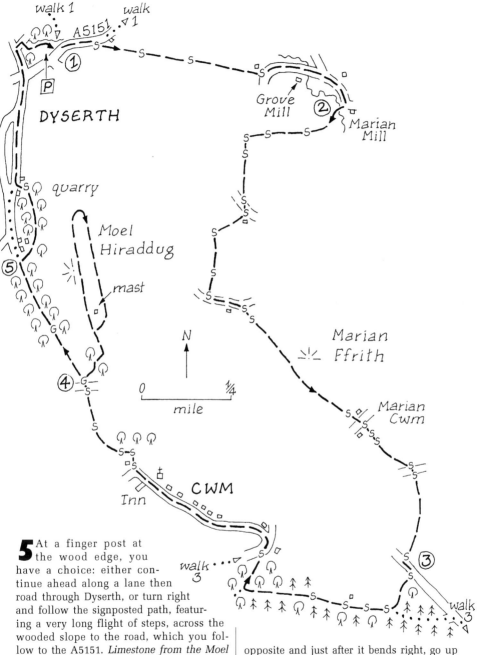

DYSERTH

quarry

Moel
Hiraddug

mast

Grove
Mill ②

Marian
Mill

Marian
Ffrith

Marian
Cwm

N

0 ———— ¼
mile

④

⑤

③

CWM

Inn

walk 3

walk 3

5 At a finger post at the wood edge, you have a choice: either continue ahead along a lane then road through Dyserth, or turn right and follow the signposted path, featuring a very long flight of steps, across the wooded slope to the road, which you follow to the A5151. *Limestone from the Moel Hiraddug quarry was burnt in limekilns here to produce lime for the chemical industry or for use as a fertilizer.* Go down Pandy Lane opposite and just after it bends right, go up stone steps on your right and follow a short woodland path, later alongside a stream, before angling up to the car park.

Walk 3

AROUND COED CWM

DESCRIPTION A 5½ mile walk exploring the attractive varied countryside between Rhuallt and Cwm, offering extensive views. The route follows field paths, passing Plas yn Cwm, and country lanes to the outskirts of Cwm. It then follows a path up through the edge of Coed Cwm to join the Offa's Dyke Path for a return down to Rhuallt. Allow about 3 hours.
START Rhuallt SJ 073751.
DIRECTIONS Park in a large lay-by opposite Jones Bros 4x4 centre and just before a bus stop and the former school, now a Special Education Centre, on the road leading west from the village crossroads.

I Go up the road and at the staggered crossroads by the Smithy Arms, take the road signposted Cwm/Dyserth. Just past the village roadsign take a signposted path over a stile on the left. Go half-RIGHT down the field – *good views to Snowdonia* – to a stile in the corner. Go along the next field edge to cross a stile/footbridge/stile in the corner. Follow the boundary on your right to a stile. Turn LEFT along the hedge/tree-lined path, then along the field/wood edge to a stile/footbridge/stile. Continue ahead, then immediately after passing through a gap in an old hedge, turn RIGHT and follow the hedge round to a stile. Now head half-LEFT across the large field – *with a good view of Plas yn Cwm* – to a stile at the end of a strip of woodland. Continue in the same direction towards a barn and cottage to go through a gate in the corner onto a road. Follow it RIGHT.

2 Shortly take a signposted path on the right along a track leading to Plas yn Cwm. Cross a stile on the left opposite a garage, then go across the field and over a stile. Keep ahead and follow the edge of the large field round past a barn in the corner, then a strip of woodland to go through a gate in the next corner. Go up the left-hand edge of the field to a stile, then up the next field to a stile in its top right-hand corner onto a minor road. Follow it LEFT – *soon enjoying extensive views across to the mountains of Snowdonia and along the coast to the Little/Great Orme*. When the road splits take the right fork and keep ahead at the next junction. Go past Cil-Haul.

3 Just before the road junction take a signposted path angling back on the right, which rises steadily across the wooded slope. After a few hundred yards, at a waymarker post, turn LEFT and follow the clear path up through the wood to a stile at the wood edge. Go up the field edge – *enjoying extensive views north to the coast, the off-shore windfarm, and Merseyside* – and cross a stile above a stone building. Continue ahead, soon following the access track to a stile. Follow the wood's perimeter fence to another stile. Keep ahead to cross the stile in the fence then follow a nearby forest track LEFT to the road. Continue along the quiet country road.

4 At the wood corner turn RIGHT along a track on the Offa's Dyke Path signposted to Rhuallt. Soon the track crosses open countryside – *with good views along the Clwydians and the Vale*. When the track bends down to a cottage, keep ahead on a green track. After a stile, keep ahead on the main green track, which makes a long gentle descent across the open hillside – *with new views of the Snowdonia mountains*. At the outbuilding of a house follow a path to a stile. Follow the path, which soon descends the gorse-covered hillside to a stile at a wood corner. From here it descends to a stile and continues down throught the wood to the road. Follow it LEFT back to Rhuallt.

6

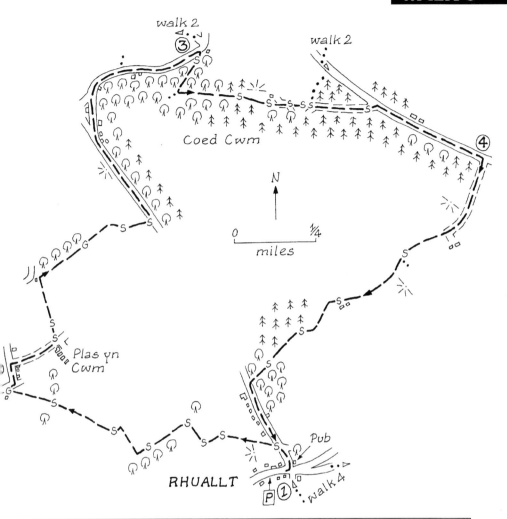

About the author, David Berry

David is an experienced walker with a love of the countryside and an interest in local history. He is the author of a series of walks guidebooks covering North Wales, where he has lived and worked for many years, as well as a freelance writer for Walking Wales magazine.

He has worked as a Rights of Way surveyor across North Wales and was a member of Denbighshire Local Access Forum.

Whether on a riverside ramble, mountain or long distance walk, he greatly appreciates the beauty, culture and history of the landscape and hopes that his comprehensive guidebooks will encourage people to explore on foot its diverse scenery and rich heritage.

Walk 4
MOEL MAENEFA

DESCRIPTION This A 5¼ mile walk (**A**) of great variety exploring the foothills of the northern Clwydians and the edge of the Vale of Clwyd, offering extensive views. After a section of the Offa's Dyke Path, the route rises across the western slopes of Moel Maenefa, featuring a prominent large wooden cross just below its summit. It follows field paths and quite country road, then descends a delightful bridleway before continuing past St. Beuno's College and following field paths back to Rhuallt. Allow about 3 hours. The route can easily be shortened to a 3 mile walk (**B**).
START Rhuallt SJ 073751. See **Walk 3**.

St. Beuno's College was built in 1848 as a college for theological students and many Jesuit priests received their final training there. It is now a Spirituality Centre and retreat for people from various countries who wish to meditate.The renowned poet Gerard Manley Hopkins studied here from 1874-77, and was ordained in the chapel. It was here that he wrote some of his major poems.

I Go up the road to the staggered crossroads by the Smithy Arms. Continue past the B5429 turning for Tremeirchion/Bodfari and the 19thC chapel, then follow Offa's Dyke Path (acorn) up the lane (no through road). At the lane end cross a long footbridge over the A55. At the other side cross a stile on the right and follow the boundary on the right down and round to stiles in the left-hand corner. Continue ahead up the field, over two stiles, then go up the next field to another stile – *good views towards Snowdonia and along the coast to the Little Orme*. Follow the path across the next field up to a waymarker post on the tree-lined ridge. Go across the next field to another waymarker post well below a ruined farm. After a stile head across the field to a stile in the right-hand corner onto a lane above St. Beuno's College. (For **Walk B** turn right.)

2 Continue up the lane and on the bend by a house, turn RIGHT to follow Offa's

Dyke Path up a bridleway. At a finger post go through the gate on the left then follow the path up the predominantly gorse-covered hillside – *enjoying great views*. About 30 yards before a gate in the fence at the top of the slope, take a path leading right to reach a large wooden cross at a prominent viewpoint just below the summit of Moel Maenefa, now a designated Open Access area. Return to the main path and follow it past the gate to cross a stile ahead. Turn RIGHT and follow a waymarked permissive path along the field edge to a stile, then LEFT down the next field edge to a stile at the entrance to houses. Follow the access track to a road.

3 Turn RIGHT along this quiet country road. At a junction, rejoin Offa's Dyke Path by turning RIGHT (signposted to Rhuallt) and follow the tree-lined bridleway past caravans. At a finger post, leave Offa's Dyke Path by continuing ahead on the bridleway – *enjoying good views along the Vale of Clwyd* – soon crossing a stile. At the bottom, just after another stile, you meet a waymarked bridleway junction. Turn RIGHT, cross a stile and continue briefly with the bridleway.

4 Cross a stile in the fence on the left. Go half-RIGHT past a low ruin and on along the bottom of the field. After a waymarked gateway head half-RIGHT across the undulating field and just before the perimeter of a wood, turn RIGHT along a path through gorse and on to cross a stile on the left. Follow the path through the wood down to rejoin the lane at point **2**. Follow it down past St. Beuno's College to the road. Cross the stile opposite and down the field past a hedge corner to go through a gate in the bottom corner. Turn LEFT along the field edge to join a track.

5 Follow it ahead through a gateway and along the next field edge to a gate. Continue along the edge of the next two long fields and after a footbridge on the left angle across the field corner to cross another footbridge. Turn RIGHT along the field edge to cross a stile/footbridge. Continue ahead to cross a larger footbridge, then follow the

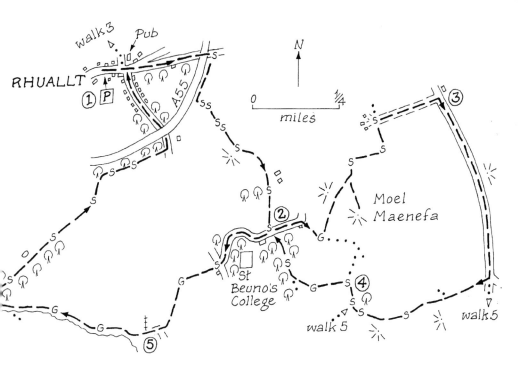

path to a stile. Go along the edge of a long field and over a stile in the corner. Go ahead across the next large field to cross a stile, then head half-LEFT towards the A55 and at a finger post, turn RIGHT along the field edge to a stile in the corner. Mid-way along the next field edge cross a stile, then follow the path to the road. Cross over and follow the road under the A55 back into Rhuallt. *Note the former British School dating from 1863 linked to the chapel built in 1835.*

Cross on Moel Maenefa

Walk 5

CEFN DDU & Y GRAIG

DESCRIPTION A 5 mile walk exploring the beautiful foothills of the northern Clwydians near Tremeirchion, offering panoramic views. The route starts from the medieval church then heads north to join Offa's Dyke Path which it follows for 1½ miles, crossing the open hillside of Cefn Ddu. It then follows a delightful bridleway down an attractive side valley to visit Y Graig, a prominent limestone crag, now a Nature Reserve, before passing caves once occupied by stone age man. Allow about 3 hours.

START Church of Corpus Christi, Tremeirchion. SJ 083731.

DIRECTIONS From Bodfari take the B5429 towards Tremeirchion. After about 2 miles, after passing Ffynnon Beuno, take a right turn, then fork up right to park alongside the church.

The attractive Church of Corpus Christi, dating mainly from the 14th and 15thC, contains many items of interest , including a 13thC cross slab forming a seat in the porch, rare 17thC portrait glass and an impressive canopied 14thC tomb. Outside stands a yew tree reputed to be over 800 years old.

I Walk up the road past the Salusbury Arms, a 14thC coaching inn, to take a signposted path through a gate on the left. Go across the field and over a stile. *Prominent on the skyline is the church of St. Beuno's College rising out of the trees.* Follow the waymarked path over two further stiles, then go half-RIGHT down the large field to cross a stile in the corner. Walk up the field ahead, close to the boundary on the right, past a stile. At the boundary corner continue down the field to cross a stream in the corner. Follow the waymarked path past a cottage to a stile, then go up the lane. At its end continue on a bridleway signposted to Moel Maenefa. When it splits, turn LEFT and follow the bridleway up over two stiles to join the signposted Offa's Dyke Path.

2 Cross the stile and follow Offa's Dyke Path angling across the hillside to a prominent viewpoint by two hawthorn trees. *Here is a good place for a break to enjoy the extensive views of the Vale of Clwyd, the coast, and the distant mountains of Snowdonia.* The path now crosses two fields, then follows a bridleway past caravans to reach a road. Turn RIGHT, still on Offa's Dyke Path. Turn LEFT at the T-junction, then RIGHT at the next and continue along the quiet country road. At the bend cross the stile ahead. Now follow Offa's Dyke Path signposted to Cefn Ddu up the field to a stile in the top fence, then across the open pasture of Cefn Ddu to another stile in the right-hand field corner, near its highest point, where you can enjoy all-round views, and on to reach a road.

3 Here you leave Offa's Dyke Path by going through a gate on your right. Now follow a bridleway between embankments, soon descending then contouring along the side valley to eventually join a lane by a house. Continue down the lane. After it bends left, turn RIGHT along a driveway (signposted to Tremeirchion/Y Graig), soon on a narrow path to enter Y Graig Nature Reserve. Turn RIGHT alongside the fence, then after about 30 yards turn LEFT up a path to reach the open limestone encrusted hilltop – *offering extensive views* – just beyond a marker post. Here turn sharp RIGHT to reach a finger post, marker post 4 and a seat.

Y Graig was bought by The North Wales Wildlife Trust with local support in 1987 to protect the ancient woodland and limestone grassland, which provide a haven for wildlife and plants. It was a favourite place for the young John Rowlands during his stays with his aunt at nearby Ffynnon Beuno, after leaving the workhouse at St. Asaph and before sailing to America in 1858 and gaining worldwide fame as the explorer H.M. Stanley. From its rocky summit he enjoyed the 'breezy freedom' and the views along the Vale, dreaming of 'the life to come'.

4 Follow the path straight ahead to pass beneath the summit crag, from where

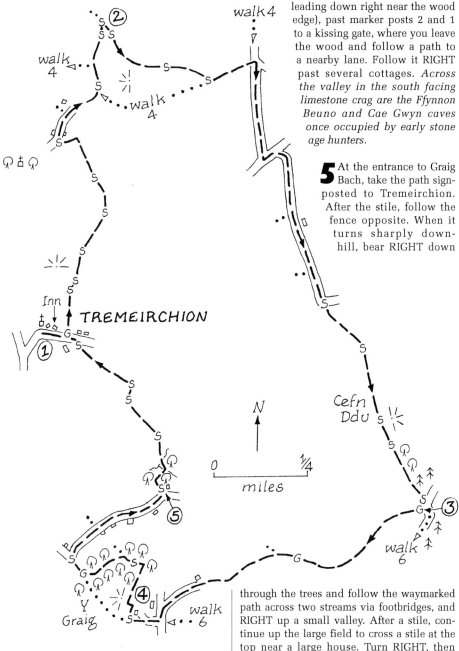

leading down right near the wood edge), past marker posts 2 and 1 to a kissing gate, where you leave the wood and follow a path to a nearby lane. Follow it RIGHT past several cottages. *Across the valley in the south facing limestone crag are the Ffynnon Beuno and Cae Gwyn caves once occupied by early stone age hunters.*

5 At the entrance to Graig Bach, take the path signposted to Tremeirchion. After the stile, follow the fence opposite. When it turns sharply downhill, bear RIGHT down

through the trees and follow the waymarked path across two streams via footbridges, and RIGHT up a small valley. After a stile, continue up the large field to cross a stile at the top near a large house. Turn RIGHT, then cross a stile on the left. Go aross the field and down steps near the corner onto the road. Turn LEFT back to the start.

it descends through the trees to a stile. The path continues down through the wood passing between two large trees (ignore a path

Walk 6

SODOM & MOEL-Y-GAER

DESCRIPTION This figure of eight 5 mile walk (**A**) explores the attractive low hills north of Bodfari, including Sodom, notable for its views and its name! The route rises in stages via quiet country roads, paths, bridleway and delightful old green lane to its most northerly point. From here it returns on the Offa's Dyke Path, passing over the open top of Cefn Ddu at 850ft, the route's highest point, and later skirting the Iron Age hillfort of Moel y Gaer. The route offers an optional visit to Y Graig nature reserve, adding ¼ mile to its length and a country inn at the finish. Allow about 3 hours The route can easily be shortened to a 2¼ mile walk (**B**).

START Maes y Graig/A541 junction, Bodfari. SJ 097701.

DIRECTIONS Maes y Graig joins the A541 by the Forge Stores, AP Motors and bus stop in Bodfari. Limited roadside parking by AP Motors.

*B*odfari, possibly the site of a Roman way-station, was once famous for St. Deifar's holy well, where it was the custom to dip children three times to prevent their crying at night. The Church of St Stephen, with its large medieval tower and fine views from the churchyard is well worth a visit.*

1 Go along Maes y Graig past the village notice-board, telephone box and houses. Shortly, the road bends right and rises out of the village, soon bending right again. It passes Tan-y-fallen, Offa's Dyke Path on the left (your return route), and a lane on the right – *with good views along the Wheeler valley and across to Moel y Parc*. Shortly after passing two further houses, the narrow road rises past woodland. Just past a waymarked Offa's Dyke Path stile on the left (your return route), when the road angles down, continue straight ahead with Offa's Dyke Path along a track.

2 At the next finger post 20 yards ahead, leave Offa's Dyke. Path by taking a narrow bridleway angling away on the right.

Follow it through the edge of woodland to a gated entrance of a house. Turn LEFT up the lane and at the junction turn RIGHT to go past Fron-Haul. At the next junction, turn LEFT and follow the road up behind the house. At the minor cross-roads, with a seat nearby, continue ahead along the quiet attractive country road – *enjoying extensive views across the Vale of Clwyd to the distant mountains of Snowdonia, and the Little Orme*. After passing three dwellings, the road continues beneath the wooded hillside. Where it begins to bend down to the left and a house, continue ahead on a signposted path through the trees and across a field to reach a lane. (Here you can link into **Walk 5**. A short diversion on the signposted path ahead to the nearby summit of Y Graig Nature Reserve is recommended.)

3 Turn RIGHT along the lane. When it bends up right, continue ahead past Pen y Graig to cross a stile by a gate and go along the old tree-lined green lane. After a gate, the green lane continues through another gate further ahead, then passes a wood on the left. After another gate and a stream, the delightful old route bends north, rising steadily up the open hillside. Near the top of the slope, it passes through a gate and continues with new views, shortly descending through an area of gorse to reach gates and stile by the bend of a road.

4 Here do a sharp U-turn and follow the Offa's Dyke Path signposted to Cefn Ddu up the field to a stile in the top fence. Continue up and across the open pasture of Cefn Ddu to a stile in the right-hand field corner, near its highest point, where you can enjoy all-round views. Follow Offa's Dyke Path to a road. Continue on the road ahead, later descending with panoramic views, to pass through the cross-roads met earlier. Further on at a T-junction, turn RIGHT, then cross a stile on the left. *This is perhaps the best close viewpoint of Moel y Gaer Iron-Age hillfort (no access). Although the lowest of the hillforts on the Clwydian range, it has formidable natural and man-made defences able to defend the population from invaders, with its entrance at the northern end.*

5 Follow the stiled Offa's Dyke Path down two fields and on to briefly join your outward route at point **2**. Continue along the road, then cross the stile on the right. Head half-LEFT up the field to cross a stile above an access track. Offa's Dyke Path soon rises beneath the eastern flanks of Moel y Gaer, passing above a house, to a stile. It then descends through the trees and contours to a stile at a good viewpoint, before descending the edge of the open slope to rejoin the road followed on your outward route. Turn LEFT, then RIGHT down the narrow lane to the A541 opposite The Downing Arms in Bodfari – *a traditional pub which makes a good end to the walk.*

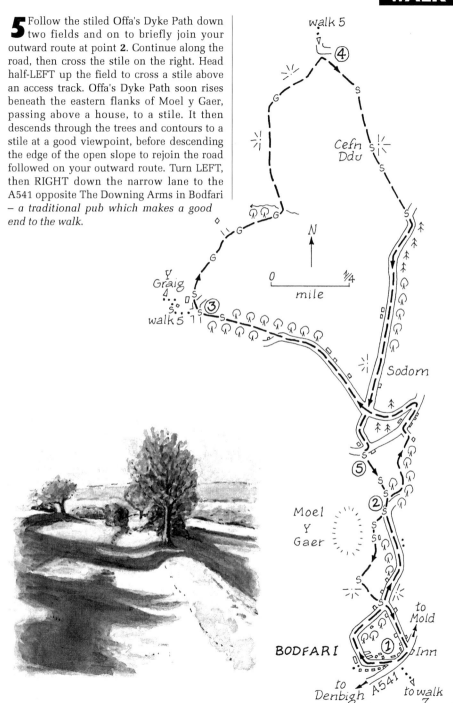

walk 5

Cefn Ddu

N

0   mile   ¼

Y Graig

walk 5

Sodom

Moel Y Gaer

BODFARI

to Mold

Inn

to Denbigh   A541   to walk 7

Walk 7
MOEL Y PARC

DESCRIPTION A 6 mile meandering walk exploring the foothills and attractive valleys near Moel-y-Parc, now a designated Open Access area, featuring delightful paths and bridleways, with panoramic views. The walk offers a choice of routes, including a climb to the 1305ft summit of Moel y Parc (**Walk A**), from where it descends to the bwlch to join the Offa's Dyke Path ascent alternative (**Walk B**). Allow about 3½ hours. The route includes alternative shorter 4 mile (**C**) or 4¾ mile (**D**) walks.
START Aberwheeler. SJ 096694.
DIRECTIONS Turn off the A541 near Bodfari on the B5429 (Llanbedr/Llandyrnog) to reach Aberwheeler after ½ mile. Just past a play area, park in a lay-by on the left, opposite 'Bro Lleweni'.

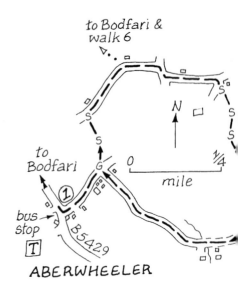

ABERWHEELER

At the nearby junction, take the side road opposite the bus stop/telephone box, Just beyond Efail-y-Waen farm, enter the field on the left opposite a lane. Go half-RIGHT to a stile, then across the next field to a road, which you follow RIGHT, soon being joined by Offa's Dyke Path. At a T-junction go RIGHT, then LEFT up a lane. *Ahead lies the bracken-covered slopes of Moel-y-Parc.* At a letter box in a facing wall, turn RIGHT on the OD. Path (signposted to Aifft) to cross a stile by Grove Goch. Follow Offa's Dyke Path to a stile in the far left-hand field corner, and along the next field edge to another stile. Now follow the waymarked stiled path angling up three fields to cross a stile by a gate and finger post.

2 Go ahead up alongside the fence on your left to a bridleway. (For a direct route up the hillside, turn right for 20 yards, then take a clear path on the left up to a prominent stone and on up the bracken/gorse-covered hillside to a small stone cairn on the top of this outlying hill. Follow the path down, keeping to the left fork, soon rising to reach a waymarker post at point **3**.) For the main

walk follow the bridleway LEFT. After a gate, continue with the enclosed bridleway to a bridleway junction. Here take the right fork angling up to a gate, and on past a small wood. After another gate, the delightful green bridleway steadily climbs the side of a little known valley, then meanders up to reach a waymarker post on the shoulder of the hill.

3 Here you have a choice. For **Walk A** turn LEFT (signposted to Moel y Parc) and follow the path up the hillside to reach a waymarker post by a small stone cairn and a fence corner on the summit of Moel y Parc, with its nearby T.V. transmitter mast. Here do a sharp U-turn and follow a path alongside the fence on a steady descent south, later passing through a small gate, before rejoining Offa's Dyke Path at a finger post by a track. (For **Walk D**, follow Offa's Dyke Path right down to point **7**.)

For **Walk B** continue ahead (signposted to Aifft) and follow the bridleway south down a valley. After a gate, continue down an access track below Fron Haul. Shortly after passing a stone cottage, the track bends left down

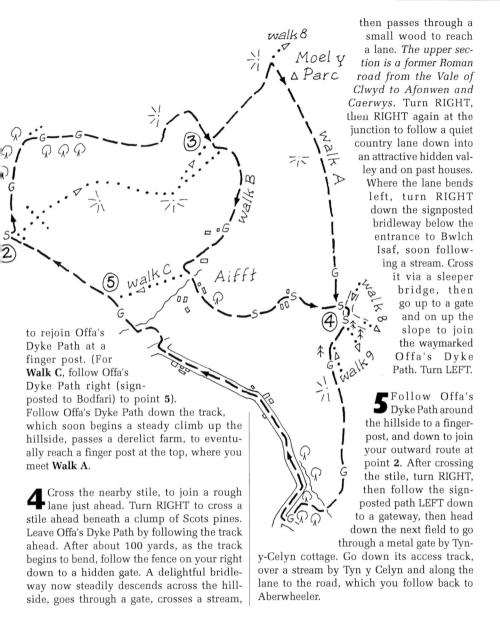

then passes through a small wood to reach a lane. *The upper section is a former Roman road from the Vale of Clwyd to Afonwen and Caerwys.* Turn RIGHT, then RIGHT again at the junction to follow a quiet country lane down into an attractive hidden valley and on past houses. Where the lane bends left, turn RIGHT down the signposted bridleway below the entrance to Bwlch Isaf, soon following a stream. Cross it via a sleeper bridge, then go up to a gate and on up the slope to join the waymarked Offa's Dyke Path. Turn LEFT.

5 Follow Offa's Dyke Path around the hillside to a finger-post, and down to join your outward route at point **2**. After crossing the stile, turn RIGHT, then follow the signposted path LEFT down to a gateway, then head down the next field to go through a metal gate by Tyn-y-Celyn cottage. Go down its access track, over a stream by Tyn y Celyn and along the lane to the road, which you follow back to Aberwheeler.

to rejoin Offa's Dyke Path at a finger post. (For **Walk C**, follow Offa's Dyke Path right (sign-posted to Bodfari) to point **5**). Follow Offa's Dyke Path down the track, which soon begins a steady climb up the hillside, passes a derelict farm, to eventually reach a finger post at the top, where you meet **Walk A**.

4 Cross the nearby stile, to join a rough lane just ahead. Turn RIGHT to cross a stile ahead beneath a clump of Scots pines. Leave Offa's Dyke Path by following the track ahead. After about 100 yards, as the track begins to bend, follow the fence on your right down to a hidden gate. A delightful bridleway now steadily descends across the hillside, goes through a gate, crosses a stream,

Walk 8
PENYCLODDIAU
&
MOEL Y PARC

DESCRIPTION An exhilarating 6½ mile walk (A) exploring the less well known areas of two prominent hills, now designated Open Access areas, offering panoramic views throughout. The route follows the Offa's Dyke Path up to the southern end of Penycloddiau before diverting to follow the western ramparts of the large Iron Age hillfort (See **Walk 9** for information) to the summit, where the Offa's Dyke Path is rejoined. Later the route follows a permissive path up to the summit of Moel y Parc with its TV. transmitter mast and down to link with a public path. The return route follows a track, then paths skirting the more remote eastern slopes of Penycloddiau, before taking a good path across the hill's south-eastern section. Allow about 3½ hours. The route can easily be shortened to a 4¼ mile circuit of Penycloddiau (**Walk B**).

START Llangwyfan Forestry car park. SJ 139668.

DIRECTIONS From the small roundabout on the B5429 north of Llandyrnog village centre, follow the side road past 'The Kimnel Arms', then at a cross-roads, turn left signposted Llangwyfan. After ½ mile, at a junction, keep ahead, and follow the minor road up the wooded valley for 1 mile to reach the forestry car park on the left at the top of the pass. Alternatively, from Mold turn off the A541 into Nannerch, then take the first road left for about 3 miles towards Llandyrnog to reach the car park.

I Go through the small gate into Coed Llangwyfan then along the forestry track to the Offa's Dyke Path waymarker post just ahead. Follow Offa's Dyke Path path up along the forest edge and past an area of cleared forest offering panoramic views. After crossing a stile continue up the southern end of Penycloddiau. After about 100 yards, leave Offa's Dyke Path Path and take a path to the nearby fence corner on the left. Follow the

clear path straight ahead across the south western section of the hillfort, with the rampart/fence down to the left. Shortly, you join the rampart which you follow past a stile and up the hillside – now with an outer rampart below – to eventually reach the summit cairn on Penycloddiau. After enjoying the extensive 360 degree views, follow the waymarked Offa's Dyke Path Path north down to a stile and across a broad green ridge towards Moel y Parc , later descending to pass a clump of Scots pines to reach a stile/gate at a green track.

2 Cross the stile. (For **Walk B** turn right to point **4**.) Continue briefly along the rough lane ahead, then turn LEFT along a green track, over a stile, and at the nearby finger post, bear RIGHT (signposted to Moel y Parc). Follow the permissive path up alongside the fence, through a small iron gate and on up to a waymarker post by the fence corner and a small stone cairn, on the summit of Moel y Parc, with an inaccessible trig point nearby. Bear RIGHT (signposted to Afonwen) and follow the wide path down towards the distant Ysceifiog lake. You pass the nearby transmitter mast and Ysceifiog lake comes back into view.

3 At a waymarker post, go through a gate on the right. Follow the fence on your right down the hillside, later through a small wood to cross a stile onto a lane. Follow it RIGHT and when it bends up towards the transmitter mast site, continue ahead along a rough track/lane, which eventually reaches your outward route. Bear LEFT with the rough lane and when it bends left towards a farm continue ahead along a green track.

4 At the end of the track go through a waymarked gate on the right and along the green track. After another gate, continue down a delightful narrowing green path into the valley beneath the bracken-covered eastern slopes of Penycloddiau to cross a stile by a gate. Continue across the reedy, occasionally wet terrain. Immediately before a stile, bear RIGHT and follow a path up the open hillside. After about 200 yards, at a facing green slope, take the path angling off to the

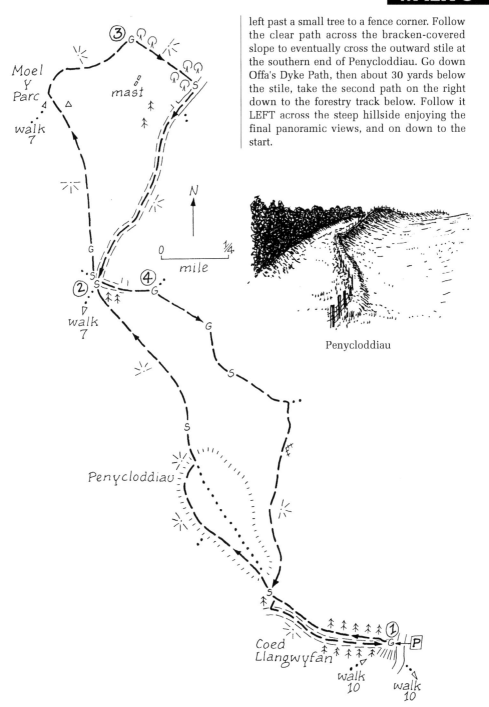

left past a small tree to a fence corner. Follow the clear path across the bracken-covered slope to eventually cross the outward stile at the southern end of Penycloddiau. Go down Offa's Dyke Path, then about 30 yards below the stile, take the second path on the right down to the forestry track below. Follow it LEFT across the steep hillside enjoying the final panoramic views, and on down to the start.

Penycloddiau

Walk 9
PENYCLODDIAU

DESCRIPTION This superb 5 mile walk, offering panoramic views, follows a forestry track, then high-level old green lane along the western flanks of Penycloddiau, before following Offa's Dyke Path up the broad ridge to its summit and across its Iron Age hillfort. One of the author's favourite walks in all seasons, and equally enjoyable in reverse direction. Allow about 2½ hours.
START Llangwyfan Forestry car park. SJ 139668. See **Walk 8**.

Penycloddiau meaning 'The hill of the trenches' is the largest Clwydian hillfort and one of the largest in Wales. Its interior is ½ mile long and it encloses an area of some 24 hectares, within a single substantial grass-covered rampart, strengthened at its northern end. There is evidence of level hut platforms within the fort.

I Go through the small gate, then along the level forestry track ahead (second from the right). Follow the track through the trees, then across the open slopes, later narrowing as it gently descends through the forest to a bridle gate. Just beyond join the old gated green lane, which you follow along the western flanks of Penycloddiau past areas of mature woodland, a large old water tank and along open slopes offering extensive views along the Vale of Clwyd.

2 After 2 miles just before a stile/gate before a rough lane, swing sharp RIGHT up the slope past a clump of Scots pines. Now simply follow the waymarked Offa's Dyke Path up to the summit of Penycloddiau, through the centre of the hillfort and on a gradual descent back to the start.

Walk 10
MOEL ARTHUR

DESCRIPTION A 4 mile walk (**A**) featuring the Iron Age hillfort on Moel Arthur, and panoramic views. The route follows the Offa's Dyke Path up to the shoulder of Moel Arthur, before diverting to its summit fort, then descends into the next valley. It returns on a bridleway down the edge of another wooded valley and around the hillside to Coed Llangwyfan. Allow about 2 hours. A shorter 3½ mile walk (**B**) using another bridleway is included.
START Llanwyfan Forestry car park. SJ 139668. See **Walk 9**. Or Moel Arthur car park. SJ 148658. See **Walk 13**.

The steep conical heather-covered hill of Moel Arthur at 1494ft is crowned by a circular Iron-Age hillfort. This small, but prominent hillfort, is defended on the naturally weaker northern side by two impressive ramparts and ditches. There is evidence of hut circles, and a hoard of Bronze Age copper axes have been found here. It offers superb 360 degree views.

I Return to the road and follow it south a short distance, then take the Offa's Dyke Path over a stile on the left. Follow the waymarked stiled path up the initially steep open slope to cross the north eastern shoulder of Moel Arthur. At a slate waymarker post, a path leads up to the top of Moel Arthur through the original fort entrance. Return to the Offa's Dyke Path and follow it down to the car park/alternative start in the next valley.

2 Follow the road over the cattle-grid and down towards the Vale of Clwyd. After nearly ½ mile, take a signposted bridleway through a gate on the right. Follow it across the head of the valley, through a gate and past a small pool, where it bends west to go through another gate. (For **Walk B**, take another bridleway angling up and across the hillside, later descending a green track. Bear left across the nearby farm's access track and follow the fence on your right down to go through a gate below the farm. Go down the field edge, then bear left and right down to a gate below. Follow the road left to join **Walk A**).

3 **Walk A** follows the bridleway down the edge of the wooded valley, around the hillside, past a partly-built house and along its access track to a road. Turn LEFT, then RIGHT on the signposted bridleway up a forestry road. (Nearby is a link path to **Walk 9**.) After 250 yards, the bridleway continues below the road, later crossing it and continuing up a track to the start.

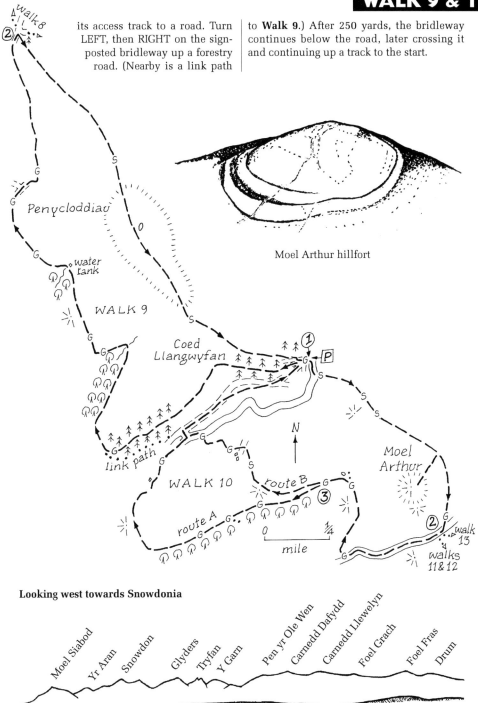

Moel Arthur hillfort

Looking west towards Snowdonia

Walk 11
THE WESTERN FLANKS

DESCRIPTION A choice of a 4½ mile (A) or 4 mile (**B**) walk, starting from a high pass, exploring the open western flanks of Moel Famau Country Park, a designated Open Access area, with panoramic views. Allow up to 2½ hours. After an initial short steep climb up Moel Llys-y-Coed, **Walk A** follows Offa's Dyke Path along the ridge, before descending a track then returning on good paths across the lower slopes, with a gradual rising track to finish. **Walk B** takes a delightful little known path across the initial mid-slopes, then follows a green track up to join the ridge path. It later descends the delighful open pasture to join **Walk A**'s return route.
START Car park beneath Moel Arthur. SJ 148658. See **Walk 13**.

1 At the nearby cattle grid cross the right of two stiles (signposted to Moel-Llys-y-coed).
Walk A Follow Offa's Dyke Path up Moel Llys-y-coed and along the ridge towards Moel Famau to point **2**.
Walk B Go up the green track leading from the Country Park sign. When it bends right, follow a path angling up the hillside. This delightful path then crosses the steep bracken-covered slope later bending south and briefly rising. At a green track, follow it LEFT up to join the Offa's Dyke Path. Follow it RIGHT to point **2**.

2 At a signposted cross-road of paths in a dip, turn RIGHT (signposted to Llangynhafal) down a part stony track. (As it starts to bend, a path angling to a nearby stile gives access to an adjoining outlying top.) Continue down the track.
Walk A Follow the stony track down the hillside to Dol-y-Caeau cottage at point **3**.
Walk B Shortly, just before two short wooden posts, go half-RIGHT down a path, soon bending towards the Vale and continuing alongside a fence to go through a gate. Follow a clear path, soon descending the

upland pasture to eventually go through a gate. Continue ahead, soon joining a short section of old sunken green track down to a waymarker post at point **4**.

3 Cross the stile below Dol-y-Caeau cottage, and follow the enclosed path to a stile and down to cross a steam. Follow the boundary to a stile. Keep ahead, then follow the waymarked path angling up the field to go through a gate by a stream. Follow the boundary on your right up past a gate to go through another gate ahead in the corner. Continue with the waymarked path.

4 Go through a gate by a ruin. Continue ahead, soon passing another ruin to cross a stream and a stile. Bear LEFT and follow the boundary on the left round past a gate, and continue with the waymarked path to join a green track. When it rises half-right, keep ahead alongside the boundary to go through a gate. Continue alongside the boundary, through another gate, to reach a lane. Go up the lane. At its end go through a gate ahead and follow the track up the valley to the start.

Walk 12
MOEL DYWYLL & MOEL FAMAU

DESCRIPTION An exhilarating 6½ mile walk following the Offa's Dyke Path along the main ridge leading to Moel Famau, then descending the attractive open hillside to return along the lower western flanks of the Clwydians. Apart from the initial short steep climb up Moel Llys-y-Coed and the final climb up Moel Famau, which is optional, the walking is steady, offering panoramic views. Allow about 3½ hours
START As **Walk 11**.

1 At the nearby cattle grid, cross the right of two stiles. Follow Offa's Dyke Path up Moel Llys-y-coed and along the ridge. After a signposted cross-road of paths (**2**) the path rises in stages across Moel Dywyll towards Moel Famau, past a prominent stone cairn/viewpoint. Shortly after pass-

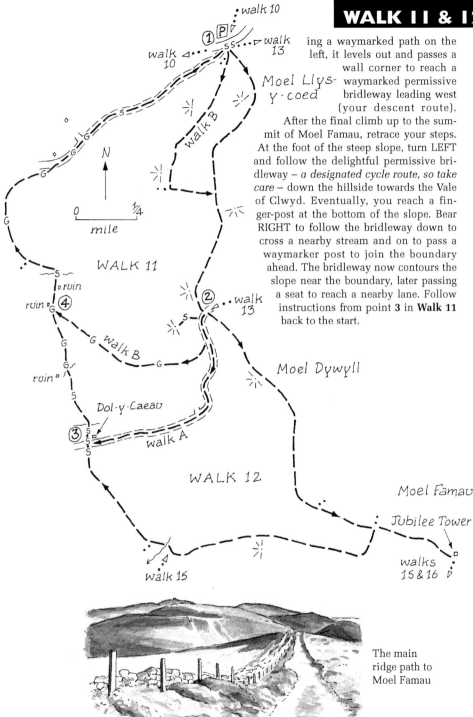

walk 10

① P

walk 10

walk 13

walk B

Moel Llys-y-coed

N

0   ¼
mile

o ruin

ruin ④

WALK 11

ruin

② walk 13

walk B

G

Moel Dywyll

Dol-y-Caeau

③

walk A

WALK 12

Moel Famau

Jubilee Tower

walk 15

walks 15 & 16

ing a waymarked path on the left, it levels out and passes a wall corner to reach a waymarked permissive bridleway leading west (your descent route).

After the final climb up to the summit of Moel Famau, retrace your steps. At the foot of the steep slope, turn LEFT and follow the delightful permissive bridleway – *a designated cycle route, so take care* – down the hillside towards the Vale of Clwyd. Eventually, you reach a finger-post at the bottom of the slope. Bear RIGHT to follow the bridleway down to cross a nearby stream and on to pass a waymarker post to join the boundary ahead. The bridleway now contours the slope near the boundary, later passing a seat to reach a nearby lane. Follow instructions from point **3** in **Walk 11** back to the start.

The main ridge path to Moel Famau

Walk 13
MOEL LLYS-Y-COED & CWM GAIN

DESCRIPTION A 5½ mile walk (A) exploring the delightful open foothills and valley scenery just north of Moel Famau, offering extensive views and the popular 16th C White Horse coaching inn mid-way for refreshments (check opening times). From the high pass beneath Moel Arthur the route crosses the northern slopes of Moel Llys-y-Coed before descending by path and quiet country lane to the attractive hillside village of Cilcain, with its splendid medieval church and inn. It then follows a bridleway along an attractive valley past reservoirs, rising steadily to join the Offa's Dyke Path back along the open ridge. Allow about 3 hours. A high level link lane/track provides a shorter 4 mile walk (B) from the car park or an easier 4¾ mile walk (C) from Cilcain.

START Car park beneath Moel Arthur [SJ 148658] An alternative start can be made from the road near waterworks ⅓ mile S.W. of Cilcain. SJ 172648.

DIRECTIONS From the small roundabout on the B5429 north of Llandyrnog village centre, follow the side road past 'The Kimnel Arms', then at a cross-roads, turn left signposted Llangwyfan. After ½ mile, turn right, then take the first road on the left up to a cattle grid and car park at the top of the pass. Alternatively, if travelling from Mold towards Denbigh on the A541, just after the turnoff to Cilcain, take the next road left up the valley to the car park beneath Moel Arthur.

Cilcain is a small hillside settlement lying beneath the eastern slopes of Moel Famau. It was listed in the Doomsday Book of 1086, and is a meeting point of old drovers roads. A visit to St. Mary's Church is highly recommended. The earliest features of the double-naved building date from the 14th and 15thC. It contains a magnificent medieval oak roof with winged angels and splendid carvings, which is believed to have been brought to the church from another building–

possibly Basingwerk Abbey – during the Dissolution of the Monasteries by Henry VIII in the early 16thC. The White Horse is the last of seven inns that once existed in the area.

1 At the nearby cattle grid cross the left of two stiles. Head LEFT across a short section of wet reedy ground, then follow the wide green path angling up across the slopes of Moel Llys-y-Coed. From the top of the rise – *with a good view of Moel Arthur* – continue ahead across the open pasture to cross a stile. Continue alongside the fence – *enjoying distant views to Cheshire, Merseyside, and the Lancashire coast* – then after a stile, descend alongside the remains of a wall to another stile. *To the south are good views of Moel Famau with its ruined Jubilee Tower.* Now follow the path along the field edge, over further stiles, down to a lane. Follow it RIGHT.

2 At cross-roads continue ahead. (For **Walk B** turn right and follow the lane to a house and continue on a delightful open track up to rejoin the main route just before the bwlch.) Follow the quiet country lane down to a junction. Turn RIGHT and follow the lane down to Cilcain. After a visit to the church and refreshments at the White Horse Inn, take the minor road on the west side of the church out of the village into open country.

3 Where the road bends sharp left past a Welsh Water Authority building (the alternative start), take the stony track on the right (a bridleway) and follow it up Cwm Gain past small reservoirs. When the track splits, go up the left fork. At a gate across the track just before the dam of another res-

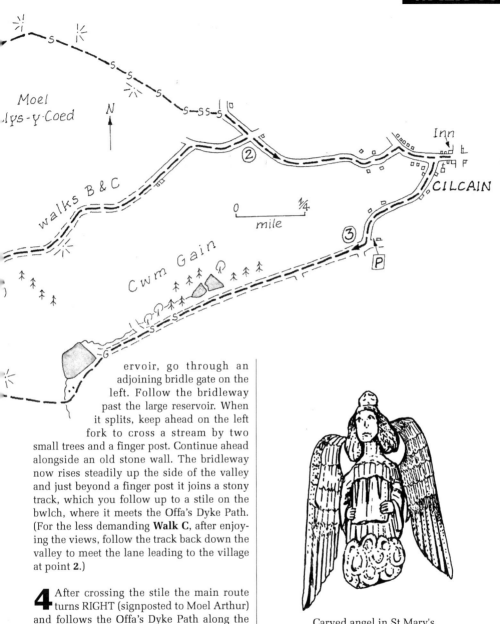

Moel
Llys-y-Coed

N

walks B & C

Cwm Gain

Inn

CILCAIN

P

0 ———— ¼
mile

② ③

ervoir, go through an adjoining bridle gate on the left. Follow the bridleway past the large reservoir. When it splits, keep ahead on the left fork to cross a stream by two small trees and a finger post. Continue ahead alongside an old stone wall. The bridleway now rises steadily up the side of the valley and just beyond a finger post it joins a stony track, which you follow up to a stile on the bwlch, where it meets the Offa's Dyke Path. (For the less demanding **Walk C**, after enjoying the views, follow the track back down the valley to meet the lane leading to the village at point **2**.)

4 After crossing the stile the main route turns RIGHT (signposted to Moel Arthur) and follows the Offa's Dyke Path along the open heather-clad ridge – *with panoramic views over the Vale of Clwyd to the coast and the mountains of Snowdonia* – later descending steeply to the road beneath Moel Arthur – *providing an excellent view of its Iron-Age hillfort.*

Carved angel in St Mary's

23

Walk 14
MOEL FAMAU

DESCRIPTION A choice of popular routes, suitable for families, through the heart of Moel Famau Country Park to the summit of Moel Famau ('Mother's mountain') – at 1820ft, the highest point in the Clwydian range – and the ruined Jubilee Tower.

START Forest car park. SJ 172611 or Moel Famau car park, Bwlch Penbarras. SJ 162606.

DIRECTIONS From Mold take the A494 towards Ruthin. After passing Loggerheads Country Park, take a minor road signposted to Moel Famau Country Park. Follow this to reach the Forest car park/toilets or continue further to the car park on the right just past a cattle grid at the top of the pass at Bwlch Penbarras. Alternative car parking is available nearby.

The tower was built in 1810 by public subscription to commemerate George 111's 50 years as king. The tower was designed by Thomas Harrison of Chester and was the first Egyptian-style monument to be built in Britain. Only the base remains, the obelisk having been blown down by storms in 1862. The 360 degree views are superb and there are viewfinding plates to help identify the many places to be seen. The remains of the Jubilee Tower are a recognised landmark seen from Cheshire and Merseyside.

From Moel Famau car park, Bwlch Penbarras

Walk A The easiest and probably most popular way to climb Moel Famau, the highest hill in the Clwydian Range, is to follow the main ridge path (Offa's Dyke Path) on a there and back 3½ mile walk from the Bwlch Penbarras car park enjoying breathtaking views throughout. Allow 1½ – 2 hours. The last section of descent can use an alternative path as shown. Although the wide path is clear, this is an exposed section.

Walk B Follow the main ridge path up to Moel Famau and descend through the forest on a choice of well waymarked trails to the Forest car park, then take a path from near the toilets above the road back to Bwlch Penbarras. The red trail is accessed via a stile just to the S.E. of Jubilee Tower. For the blue trail, which is longer but less steep, briefly return down the ridge path to find its start on the left. For the 3½ or 4 mile walk allow 2 – 3 hours.

From the Forest car park

Walk C From the large information board near the stream, follow either the waymarked red or longer but less steep blue trail to the summit. Return by the same or the alternative trail. For the 2¼ or 3¼ mile walk allow 1½ – 2 hours.

Walk D Follow either of the waymarked red or blue trails to the summit. Return down the main ridge (Offa's Dyke Path) to Bwlch Penbarras. Go left through the first car park to a kissing gate and follow the path above the road back. For the 3½ or 4 mile walk allow 2 – 3 hours.

Walk E Follow either of the waymarked red or blue trails to the summit. Return down the main ridge (Offa's Dyke Path), then take the nearby path initially running alongside the forest. It then bends east and descends to a forest track. Keep ahead, past pools, then at the track junction bear right. Shortly take a waymarked path on the left through the trees down to the car park. For the 2¾ or 3¼ mile walk allow about 1½ – 2 hours.

Jubilee Tower

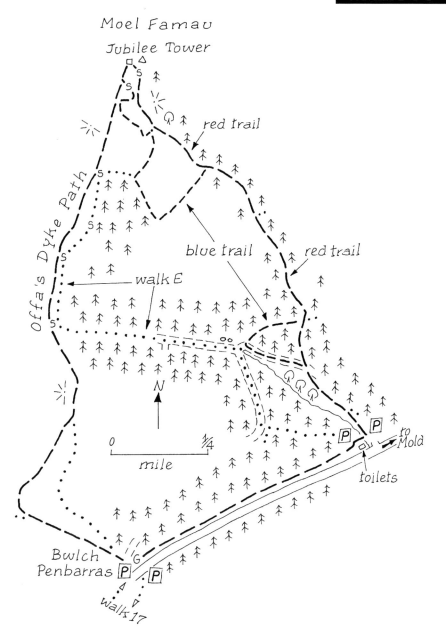

Moel Famau
Jubilee Tower
red trail
Offa's Dyke Path
blue trail
red trail
walk E
N
0   ¼
mile
to Mold
toilets
Bwlch
Penbarras
walk 17

Walk 15
MOEL FAMAU VIA ITS WESTERN FLANKS

DESCRIPTION A 5¼ mile walk for more experienced walkers, leaving the crowds behind in a circuitous route to Moel Famau, exploring the western flanks of Moel Famau Country Park and enjoying extensive views. The route first descends the open hillside, then follows a waymarked path beneath Moel y Gaer and along the lower slopes, before following a delightful permissive bridleway back up to join the Offa's Dyke Path for a short climb up to the summit of Moel Famau and a descent to the start. Allow about 3½ hours.
START Moel Famau car park, Bwlch Penbarras. SJ 162606. See **Walk 14**.

I From the car park take the wide stony Offa's Dyke Path (signposted to Jubilee Tower). Shortly, at a finger post, take a path angling down on the left to cross a stile and continue to a waymarker post. Go half-RIGHT down the bracken/bilberry covered slope to cross a ladder stile – *with a view of the heather and bracken covered side ridges of the western Clwydians stretching out like extended fingers, and the isolated hillfort of Moel-y-Gaer.* Bear LEFT down a green track and after 25 yards as it curves left, follow a faint path down the open pasture aiming to cross the right shoulder of the small gorse-capped hill ahead. The increasingly clear path then angles down the hillside to a stile then follows the fence on the left down to the bottom corner. Here, swing sharp RIGHT along a green track leading to a delightful side valley.

2 At a waymarker post turn LEFT down to cross a stile. Continue ahead down to cross a footbridge and a nearby stile. Go past a cottage, then take the waymarked path up the right fork of an access track. Shortly after a cattle grid, when the track angles down, keep ahead on the waymarked path to cross a stile above Fron Goch, Go half-RIGHT up the field past a waymarker post to another in the top corner. Continue above a tree boundary to a waymarker post and on ahead to a gate.

3 Continue ahead, soon descending the open slope past a waymarker post to another. Here bear LEFT to follow a path near a fence through an area of gorse to go through a gate. Cross the stream and follow the waymarked path LEFT along the edge of the small bracken-covered valley, later veering away to join a boundary by trees enclosing a cottage. Follow the boundary across the lower slopes.

4 At a waymark post, where the wall descends to a stream, go half-RIGHT up to a finger post. Now follow the delightful permissive bridleway – *a designated cycle route, so take care* – up the attractive hillside to eventually reach the Offa's Dyke Path running along the main ridge of Moel Famau. Follow Offa's Dyke Path up to the summit of Moel Famau, then down, with a later alternative path option, to the start.

Walk 16
MOEL-Y-GAER & MOEL FAMAU

DESCRIPTION A short but demanding 4¼ mile walk for more experienced walkers exploring the western flanks of Moel Famau Country Park, a designated Open Access area, featuring the most remote of the Clwydian Iron Age hillforts and extensive views throughout. The route descends to the base of Moel-y-Gaer, for a short steep climb to its summit, with an optional link to Walk 15, then follows paths across the bracken, bilberry and heather-covered slopes up to Moel Famau, returning down the Offa's Dyke Path. Allow about 3 hours.
START As **Walk 15**.

Moel-y-Gaer *is a classic contour fort with a double circuit of ramparts, strength-*

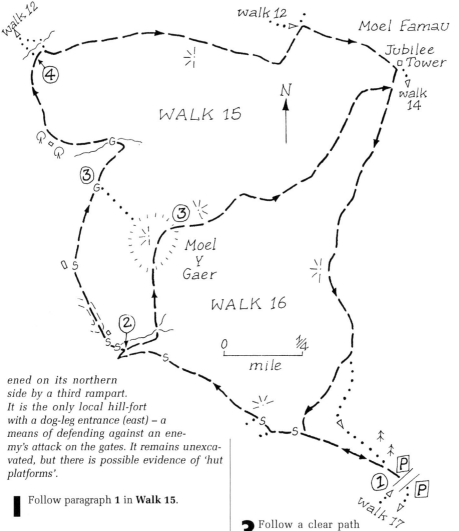

WALK 15

WALK 16

Moel Famau

Jubilee Tower

walk 12

walk 12

walk 14

walk 17

Moel Y Gaer

N

0   ¼
mile

ened on its northern side by a third rampart. It is the only local hill-fort with a dog-leg entrance (east) – a means of defending against an enemy's attack on the gates. It remains unexcavated, but there is possible evidence of 'hut platforms'.

1 Follow paragraph **1** in **Walk 15**.

2 Go past a waymarker post and follow the green track to its end. Just before a large rockface cross the stream and go up through the bracken to a small crag above. Now follow a clear path up the steep bracken/gorse-covered southern slope of Moel-y-Gaer to cross two sections of the hillfort's ramparts. Continue up across the open top of Moel-y-Gaer to its north-eastern corner. (A stile below its north-western corner allows you to descend the open slope to join **Walk 15** at a gate in the boundary on the left at point **3**.)

3 Follow a clear path heading east across the bracken/bilberry terrain, parallel with the fence on the left. It then steadily rises towards the Moel Famau ridge to eventually level out, where it heads towards the Jubilee Tower, shortly rising through a fire break in the heather. After a second cross fire break, the tower disappears. Keep ahead and soon the path bends up to join the ridge path leading up to the top of Moel Famau. Return down the Offa's Dyke Path, with a later alternative path option, to the start.

Walk 17

MOEL FENLLI & CWM BLAENNANT

DESCRIPTION A 6¼ mile walk (**A**) of great variety, with excellent views. The route visits the impressive Iron-Age hill-fort of Moel Fenlli before meandering in open country with Offa's Dyke Path to Clwyd Gate, then returning through the little known western fringes of the Clwydians, featuring attractive woodland and the delightful hidden valley of Cwm Blaennant. Allow about 3½ hours. The route includes an alternative 2½ mile walk (**B**). Initially there are a choice of routes: a short steep climb to the summit of Moel Fenlli (**a**) or the Offa's Dyke Path which climbs more steadily across the hillside before contouring round the hillfort's ramparts (**b**). Combining both makes an excellent short Moel Fenlli 1 mile walk.

START Moel Famau car park at Bwlch Penbarras. SJ 162606.

DIRECTIONS From Mold take the A494 towards Ruthin. Shortly after passing Loggerheads Country Park, take a minor road signposted to Moel Famau Country Park. Follow this road for 2 miles, past a car park/ toilets, to reach a car park on the left at the top of the pass. An alternative car park is on the right.

*M*oel Fenlli is an impressive hillfort with double ramparts defending the north and east of the hill, with its main entrance on the west side. The fort had a good supply of water from its own spring and from ones nearby. The views are breathtaking: from Merseyside to Cader Idris; from the coast to the Berwyns; from Snowdonia to Cheshire.

I Route a: For the climb to the top of the hillfort, go to the far end of the car park, then take a path signposted to Foel Fenlli through a kissing gate. The stiled path zig-zags up the northern heather-covered slope of Moel Fenlli to the highest rampart of the hillfort, then continues to the summit cairn. Head south to rejoin the rampart then bear RIGHT to follow a path angling steadily down the hillside to join the Offa's Dyke Path at a waymark post at point **2**. Turn LEFT. **Route b**: From the road by the cattle grid, follow the less demanding, but delightful, Offa's Dyke Path (signposted to Clwyd Gate) to point **2**.

2 Follow Offa's Dyke Path as it skirts the southern flanks of the hill before descending to cross a stile. (For **Walk B** turn RIGHT and follow a good path on a steady descent along the edge of Cwm Blaennant, keeping just below the fence. The path eventually bends away from the valley to a stile. Continue across the field past a waymarker post to another stile and the nearby road. Follow it RIGHT up the edge of attractive Cwm Ceunant back to the start.) For **Walk A** continue on the stiled path past the end of a forest into a field. The path now heads half-LEFT to follow the fence to a stile in the far corner and continues past a wood and along the field edge. In the corner turn RIGHT, and follow the waymarked Offa's Dyke Path through two fields, the edge of a wood, a narrow field then along a track to the A494. Turn RIGHT then cross this busy road WITH CARE. Just beyond the entrance to the Clwyd Gate Motel, angle down a lane.

3 On the bend, you leave Offa's Dyke Path, by crossing a stile on your right. Keep ahead down the field to a stile and continue through the edge of a small wood, then down a track to a cottage. Follow the waymarked stiled path past the cottage and continue through delightful woodland to enter a field. Go down the field to a stile in the hedge ahead, then go half-RIGHT down the next field. Mid-way, head towards a waymarked gate in the boundary on the right. After crossing a stream, the path turns RIGHT up the edge of a wooded valley to a lane. Follow it LEFT up to the A494. Turn LEFT and walk along the grass verge for about 100 yards, then cross the road WITH CARE to take a signposted path up a track opposite.

4 Follow the track past a wood and the entrance to Cae-Mawr farm. After passing above outbuildings, continue on a delightful old green track along the attractive

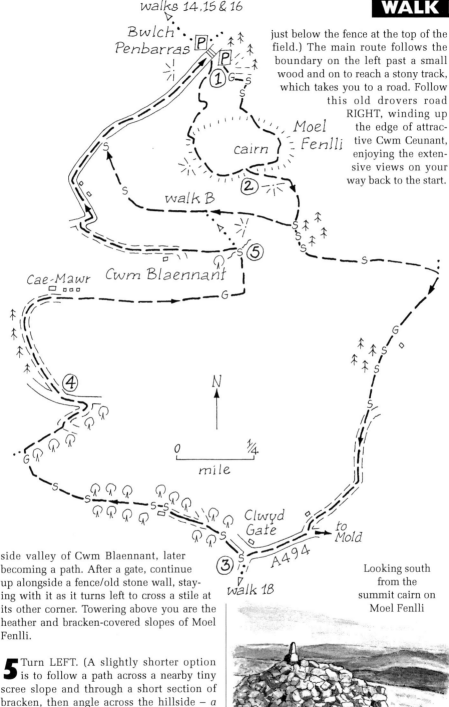

walks 14,15 & 16

Bwlch
Penbarras

Moel
Fenlli

cairn

walk B

Cae-Mawr   Cwm Blaennant

N

0   ¼
mile

Clwyd
Gate

to
Mold

A494

walk 18

just below the fence at the top of the field.) The main route follows the boundary on the left past a small wood and on to reach a stony track, which takes you to a road. Follow this old drovers road RIGHT, winding up the edge of attractive Cwm Ceunant, enjoying the extensive views on your way back to the start.

Looking south
from the
summit cairn on
Moel Fenlli

side valley of Cwm Blaennant, later becoming a path. After a gate, continue up alongside a fence/old stone wall, staying with it as it turns left to cross a stile at its other corner. Towering above you are the heather and bracken-covered slopes of Moel Fenlli.

5 Turn LEFT. (A slightly shorter option is to follow a path across a nearby tiny scree slope and through a short section of bracken, then angle across the hillside – *a designated open access area* – to join **Walk B**

29

Walk 18

MOEL GYW & COED PLAS-Y-NANT

DESCRIPTION A 6 mile walk exploring the open hills, offering panoramic views, and two quiet side valleys on the fringe of the Vale of Clwyd. Starting from an ancient high pass through the Clwydians, the route follows Offa's Dyke Path up to skirt the flanks of Moel Gyw and Moel Llanfair, and includes the new opportunity to visit the summit of Moel Gyw (1532ft), now a designated Open Access area. It then descends via track and lane into the Vale of Clwyd before returning on a bridleway up through the attractive mixed woodland of Coed Plas-y-Nant. Allow about 3 hours.

START Clwyd Gate Motel. SJ 164582]

DIRECTIONS The Clwyd Gate Motel lies at the top of the pass on the A494 Mold – Ruthin road about 3 miles from Ruthin, overlooking the Vale of Clwyd. Parking is allowed in the Motel car park, by kind permission of the owner. Please notify the Motel reception upon arrival.

1 Cross the A494 WITH CARE. Turn RIGHT, then angle down a lane, now on Offa's Dyke Path (signposted to Moel Gyw). It soon becomes a track and passes houses and another track leading to a farm. After a stile the OD. Path rises up two fields, then crosses the westerrn flanks of Moel Gyw', with panoramic views along the Vale of Clwyd from the coast to the Llantisilio Mountains.

2 Eventually you reach a multiple finger post. Take the path signposted to Moel Gyw to a nearby track. *Along the track to the right is a large stone known as ' Garreg Lwyd' (Grey Stone) marking an ancient route over the hills between Ruthin and Llanarmon-yn-ial.* Follow the track LEFT to a large slate marker, from where a clear path takes you to the trig point on the summit of Moel Gyw. After enjoying the views retrace your steps to the finger post. Now continue with the Offa's Dyke Path to a stile then down a track

to cross a stile on the left, and on across the mid-slopes of Moel Llanfair to reach a stony track.

3 Turn RIGHT down the track, soon bending RIGHT and following the track down the edge of a wide valley to houses. Continue down the lane past Sinet – *note the dovecot and weather vane* – to a junction. Turn RIGHT to reach another main junction, then turn RIGHT along the road towards Llanbedr.

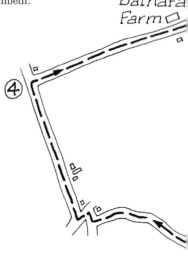

4 After ½ mile, turn RIGHT on a bridleway along a lane leading to 18thC Bathafarn Farm. *Ahead on the hills can be seen your high-level outward route.* Go past the farm. *To the left you will see Bathafarn Hall, believed to date from the early 18thC.* Continue up the lane past waterworks. When it bends left at Plas-y-nant Lodge, continue ahead up a track through Coed Plas-y-Nant,. The track rises through the mixed woodland, passing a side track, then a stone barn at the head of the valley to eventually leave wood. Simply follow the track to join your outward route.

30

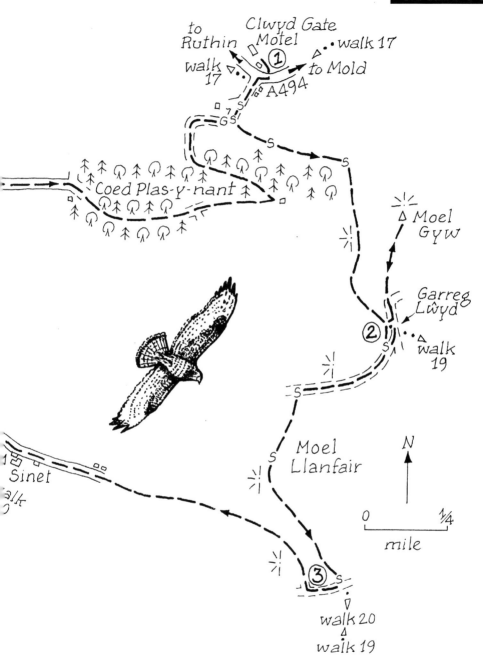

to Ruthin

Clwyd Gate Motel

① ·· walk 17

walk 17

to Mold

A494

G S

Coed Plas-y-nant

△ Moel Gyw

Garreg Lŵyd

② walk 19

Moel Llanfair

Sinet

N

0 ¼ mile

③

walk 20

walk 19

Walk 19
LLYN GWERYD & MOEL GYW

DESCRIPTION This 5½ mile walk (**A**), offering panoramic views, rises steadily to the attractive upland lake of Llyn Gweryd, then follows a delightful section of Offa's Dyke Path across Moel y Plas and beneath Moel Llanfair. After a short diversion to the summit of Moel Gyw (1532ft), now a designated Open Access area, the walk returns across the attractive green eastern flanks of the Clwydians. Allow about 3 hours. The route includes alternative 4¾ mile (**B**) and 4¼ mile (**C**) walks utilising a quiet country lane.

START St. Garmon Church, Llanarmon-yn-ial. SJ 191561.

DIRECTIONS From the A494 Ruthin-Mold road, take the B5430 towards Llanarmon-yn-ial, and after 2 miles turn right on the B5431 to enter the village. Go past the C18th Raven Inn, and as the main road swings left, continue straight ahead to park on the roadside in Maes Ial.

*B*efore starting the walk, a visit to the Church of St. Garmon is highly recommended. This fascinating medieval double-naved church, extensively restored during the 1730s, has many outstanding features. One of its finest items is a brass chandelier made in Bruges in about 1500.

I From the church's side entrance, take the path opposite, signposted to Nurse Fawr. The path passes between gardens, then continues ahead through a small housing estate. At the bottom, take the enclosed path past the right-hand side of no. 17 to cross a stile into a field. Turn RIGHT and follow the stiled path along the edge of two fields, then angle across the next field to a road. (For **Walk B**, turn right, then take the next lane on the left up to rejoin the main route at point **3**.) Go up the lane opposite on the signposted bridleway, past nearby Plas Farm. The lane/track rises steadily, then briefly bends south before continuing past a house overlooking a series of fish pools.

2 Just beyond its outbuilding cross a stile up on the right in the conifers and one just above. Follow a path LEFT past the forest and on across the bracken/heather covered hillside overlooking Llyn Gweryd to cross an old stile at the wood corner. Continue ahead briefly alongside the fence, then angle away from the wood to reach Offa's Dyke Path. Follow it RIGHT to a ladder-stile and up the hillside to a stile and on across Moel y Plas, passing above a heather-covered side valley, soon descending to a track. Turn LEFT. (For **Walk C** turn right and follow the lane down to a road junction and back to Llanarmon.)

3 Cross the stile on the right (signposted to Clwyd Gate). Follow the delightful Offa's Dyke Path across the mid-slopes of Moel Llanfair – *enjoying extensive views along the Vale of Clwyd and towards Snowdonia* – then up a track to cross a stile just below the bwlch, and on to reach a wide green path at a multi-finger post, where you leave the Offa's Dyke Path. Turn RIGHT, then immediately take the path signposted to Moel Gyw to a nearby track. Follow it LEFT to a large slate marker, from where a clear path rises to the trig point on Moel Gyw's summit. After enjoying the all-round views, return to the track and follow it back for about 140 yards to a large stone – *'Garreg Lwyd' (grey stone)* – marking an ancient route between Ruthin and Llanarmon .

4 Here take a path angling half-LEFT to cross a ladder-stile and one ahead. Bear LEFT along the field edge to another stile and continue along the delightful green ridge, near the fence, soon descending – *with views down to Llanarmon* – then angling half-RIGHT down to a stile. Go down the next field to a stile, then down through bracken to another stile. Just below, near a cottage, turn LEFT and follow the fence on your right down and round to an access drive. Follow it past a small pond, then on a bend cross a stile and head half-RIGHT to a stile onto a road. Continue ahead past the nearby chapel and follow the road back to Llanarmon.

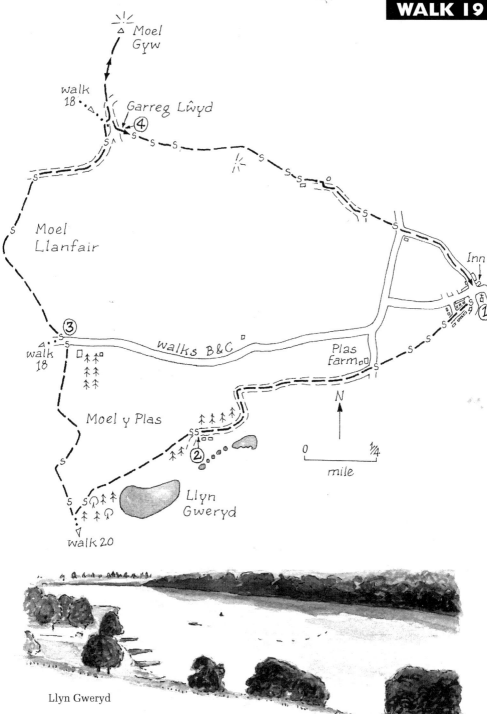

Moel Gyw

walk 18

Garreg Lŵyd
④

Moel Llanfair

Inn

①

③
walk 18

walks B&C

Plas farm

Moel y Plas

②

N

Llyn Gweryd

0   ¼
mile

walk 20

Llyn Gweryd

Walk 20
MOEL Y PLAS

DESCRIPTION This 5 mile walk (**A**) or slightly shorter alternative walk (**B**) explores the attractive western edges of the Clwydians near Graigfechan. The route, using paths, green tracks and quiet lanes, features woodland, limestone, a small lake, scenic side valleys, a delightful short section of Offa's Dyke Path over Moel y Plas, at just over 1300 feet, offering panoramic views, and refreshments at an old drovers inn at the finish (check opening times). Allow about 3 hours.

START The Three Pigeons Inn, Graigfechan. SJ 147544.

DIRECTIONS The Inn lies on the northern edge of Graigfechan village on the B5429. Parking is allowed in its car park, but the landlord will appreciate being informed.

The Three Pigeons Inn was once an important stopping place for drovers moving livestock from the Vale of Clwyd to markets further afield. Several small quarries also worked the nearby hillside to extract limestone for building material, and for lime, an important fertiliser, produced in kilns.

I Walk south down the road, then turn LEFT along a track on a signposted bridleway. After 20 yards, leave the track and follow the signposted bridleway on the left up to another track. Follow it LEFT to pass a house, then continue on a path through the trees to cross a stile just beyond another house, with a disused limekiln nearby. Continue with the woodland path alongside the boundary.

2 At a waymark post, just before a field, head half-RIGHT up to another waymarker post. Continue ahead on a path just inside the wood boundary, later crossing a wooden fence, after which the tree-lined path descends to emerge in the adjoining field corner. Go ahead down a short tree-lined green track past a house to cross a stile up on the right. Follow the boundary on the left to another stile and a road. Follow the road LEFT between cottages and past Plas Tirion.

3 Just before a road junction, take the signposted path through a gate on the right. Follow the boundary on your left round past a gate to go through another. Continue ahead along the field edge to cross a stile in the corner (can be muddy) to reach a small lake – *created as a haven for wildlife, including swans, coots and other waterfowl.* Bear RIGHT to follow a path over a small footbridge, through the trees and on to cross a stile into a field. Go up the left-hand field edge and just before the house boundary, follow the waymarked path LEFT to a stile in the corner. Cross a sleeper bridge just before the house entrance and follow the path up to a stile, and on up to a gate and a lane by the entrance to Sinet Farm. *Note the small dovecot.* Follow the lane up to cottages, then continue on a green track up the edge of the valley to reach the top of the pass, crossed by Offa's Dyke Path.

4 Cross the stile on the right and follow Offa's Dyke Path (Llandegla) up over the flanks of Moel-y-Plas and down to a ladder-stile – *enjoying good views of Llyn Gweryd and the southern Clwydians.* Continue ahead. (**Walk B**: After about 120 yards go half-right to join and follow a path down a side valley, then follow quiet lanes back to Graigfechan.) The main route passes the transmitter mast, then descends to reach a minor road.

5 At the entrance to Pen-y-Ffrith Fishery, you leave Offa's Dyke Path by taking the signposted path over a stile on the right Follow a delightful green track along the edge of the attractive side valley. Later, when the track splits, keep to the lower fork to reach a lane by Pen-y-Bryn Farm. Follow it down, and just past Bryn Dibyn cross a stile on the right. Keep ahead alongside the hedge for 100 yards, then angle down the field to cross a stile in the corner. Head down towards houses to a stile, then follow the enclosed path between houses and on to reach the road. Follow it LEFT past houses to a T-junction. Turn RIGHT along the road to the start and a relaxing drink at the inn.

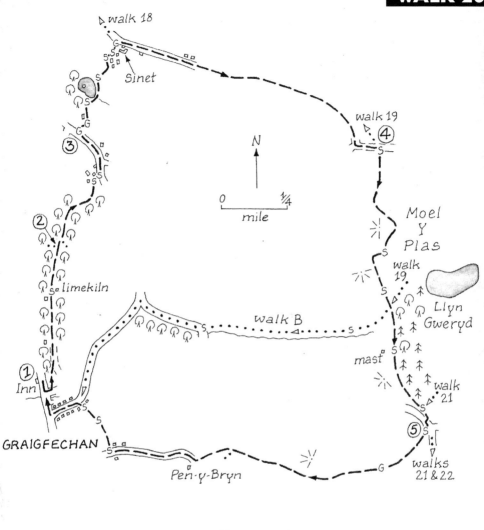

△ walk 18

Sinet

③

②

limekiln

①
Inn

GRAIGFECHAN

Pen-y-Bryn

N

0   ¼
    mile

walk 19
△ ④

Moel
Y
Plas

walk
19

Llyn
Gweryd

mast

walk
21

⑤

walks
21 & 22

walk B

Walk 21
LLYN GWERYD & LIMESTONE PASTURES

DESCRIPTION A 6 mile walk exploring the delightful varied countryside around Llanarmon-yn-ial. The route rises across the gentle green eastern flanks of the Clwydians to Gweryd lake in its wooded hillside setting, then follows a section of the Offa's Dyke Path, before returning through a wooded limestone area, past the remains of a 11thC fortress and an ancient cave. Allow about 3½ hours.
START St. Garmon Church, Llanarmon-yn-ial [SJ 191561].
DIRECTIONS From the A494 Ruthin-Mold road, take the B5430 towards Llanarmon-yn-ial, and after 2 miles turn right on the B5431 to enter the village. Go past the C18th Raven Inn, and as the main road swings left, continue straight ahead to park on the roadside in Maes Ial.

Before starting the walk, a visit to the Church of St. Garmon is highly recommended. This fascinating medieval double-naved church, extensively restored during the 1730s, has many outstanding features. One of its finest items is a brass chandelier made in Bruges in about 1500.

I From the church's side entrance, take the path opposite, signposted to Nurse Fawr. The path passes between gardens, then continues ahead through a small housing estate. At the bottom, take the enclosed path past the right-hand side of no. 17 to cross a stile into a field. Turn RIGHT and follow the stiled path along the edge of two fields, then angle across the next field to a road. Go up the lane opposite on the signposted bridleway, past nearby Plas Farm. The lane/track rises steadily, then briefly bends south before continuing past a house overlooking a series of fish pools.

2 Follow the track past a fishing office/ shop/cafe then past the end of Llyn Gweryd – *a popular fishing lake that became a reservoir about 1870* – and the mixed woodland of Nurse Fawr to eventually go through a gate to join the Offa's Dyke Path, which takes you to a nearby road – *with good views looking west down a side valley towards the Vale of Clwyd.* Follow the road up the hillside and down to cross a stile on the left. Follow the waymarked stiled Offa's Dyke Path path through a series of fields down to a farm driveway.

3 Here leave the Offa's Dyke Path, by crossing the stile opposite. Go ahead along the field edge to a stile in the corner and across the next field to another stile. Head half-RIGHT, soon passing above an old limekiln and down to cross a stile by a stream in the recessed field corner. *Lime-kilns are a feature of this area, and the lime produced was used by local farmers as a fertiliser.* Go past the nearby stile and through an old gateway. Now go half-RIGHT across a large field towards the left-hand edge of a small wood ahead.

4 Mid-way, turn RIGHT towards the field corner to cross a stile and large footbridge over the steam. Go half-LEFT up the field to a stile, then follow the path through the small wood to enter a large field. Head down the field to a bridle gate by the boundary to the right of a large barn and continue to a stile onto a road. Follow it RIGHT. After about 250 yards, take a signposted bridleway on the left, at first enclosed. After crossing a footbridge, keep ahead (can be muddy), through a gate and across a farm track to go through a bridle gate. The bridleway skirts a farm and woodland, passes through a gate, then rises up the field edge. *The nature of the land begins to change with the appearance of exposed limestone.*

5 At a metal gate on your right, leave the bridleway and head half-LEFT up the limestone-decked slope to cross a stile in a wall corner, to unexpectedly land on a golfing green. The next section passes through a small discrete golf course set amongst

36

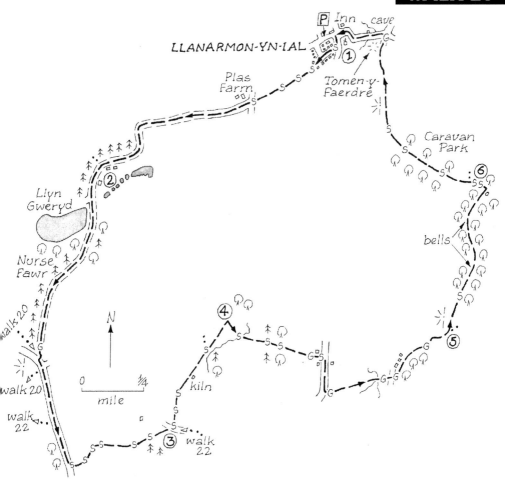

delightful tree-covered exposed limestone ridges. Keep to the field boundary on the left, past a warning bell to alert golfers, and on up between wooded ridges, soon descending past another bell. After passing a small pool at the bottom of the slope, bear LEFT to cross a stile in the corner and another just ahead.

6 Continue ahead past a stile and on alongside a caravan park boundary soon descending to cross a ladder-stile. Keep ahead, shortly passing through an old gateway and on to another large ladder-stile. Continue along the field edge to a stile in the

corner, and on along the remains of an old green lane – *once an important road used to convey people by carriage to Llanarmon Church* – to reach the road. Nearby are the remains of Tomen-y-Faerdre – *a medieval fortress, possibly 11thC in origin. The mound or 'motte' forms part of a natural rock outcrop overlooking the river Alun, and defended on the other sides by an artificial ditch. It originally supported a stone tower or 'bailey'. Ahead is a large cave where prehistoric remains have been found.* Follow the road LEFT back to the start.

Walk 22
THE ALUN VALLEY & MOEL Y WAUN

DESCRIPTION This delightful 7 mile walk from the old drovers village of Llandegla explores the attractive Alun valley and the open slopes of Moel y Waun, now partly a designated Open Access area. It features fine contrasting scenery, a medieval fortress and extensive views. Allow about 4 hours.

START Church of St. Tegla, Llandegla SJ 196524.

DIRECTIONS There is a car park in Llandegla opposite the Memorial Hall, just before the church.

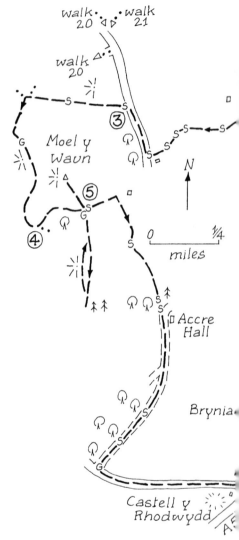

*T*he 19thC church contains many interesting items including a medieval brass chandelier, an old font, and a Georgian window made in 1800 for St. Asaph Cathedral.

I Take the signposted Offa's Dyke Path down a track between the church and the old rectory and on along the edge of a large field to cross a footbridge over the river Alun. The path now follows the boundary on the right to a stile just before the field corner, then continues along the field edge, past the end of a small wood and on to cross a footbridge. It then briefly accompanies the river.

2 As the river bends away keep ahead to cross a stile. Turn LEFT then RIGHT to follow the right-hand edge of a large field. At its corner, turn LEFT and follow the path to a road. *Nearby are several caves, once occupied by early man.* Go up the track opposite towards Chweleiriog Llwyd. *In a field on the left is St. Garmon's Well, once known for its healing properties.* As the track eventually begins to rise towards the farm, follow Offa's Dyke Path up through a series of fields to a road. Turn RIGHT up the road, then leave Offa's Dyke Path by crossing a stile on the left.

3 Pass to the right of trees ahead and go down the slope to a stile near the fence corner. Continue ahead down the path, then at a stile, turn LEFT up a green track, which takes you around the western flanks of Moel y Waun, passing through a gate into open access land – *enjoying panoramic views.*

4 At a gate in the adjoining fence, where the track begins to bend left into a side valley, head LEFT up the slope towards a small aerial on the top of Moel y Waun, to a fence corner above trees. Follow the track up to the ridge. Just before a stile in the fence marking the end of open access, a short climb left will take you past the aerial to the summit trig point to enjoy the extensive views. Return to the stile. (For a further exploration of the Moel y Waun ridge, go through the gate below the stile

lk 21

°*St Garmon's well*

Erw-o Fawr

caves

②

River Alun

⑥

St Tegla's well

LLANDEGLA

Ⓟ

and follow a faint track beneath the boundary to its highest point by a strip of woodland. Retrace your steps, then take the left fork of the track, soon joining your outward track back to the gate.)

5 Cross the stile and head down towards a house. At the fence turn RIGHT and follow the old field boundary. Before its end angle half-RIGHT up to a stile. Continue ahead, then angle down to the boundary which you follow down to cross two stiles. Go along a tree-lined track behind Accre Hall and follow it down to a road. Follow it LEFT to a junction. *Just past a 'Give-Way' sign,*

on your right is Castell y Rhodwydd – one of the finest medieval motte and bailey castles in Wales, built by Owain Gwynedd during his conquest of northern Powys in 1149. It occupies an important strategic position controlling the Nant-y-Garth pass through the Clwydians. Turn LEFT on the B5431, and after passing the entrance to Bryniau – *where an ancient cutting stone tool originating from Penmaenmawr was found in 1922 –* cross a stile on the right. Head half-LEFT across the field to a gate and straight on across the next field to another gate at a minor road.

6 Turning right will take you direct to Llandegla, but a more interesting route is to turn LEFT. At a junction, follow the road RIGHT, and just before the entrance to Erw-fawr, cross a stile on the right. Go ahead, soon bending LEFT and follow the waymarked path past a corrugated shed, over a green track and down to a grassy shelf. Descend the slope and go half-LEFT to a stile and on to another stile beyond a small rise. Continue half-LEFT to a way-marker post, then follow the fence on your left. Just past a derelict cottage above you, angle up to a waymark post. At another waymarker post on a low ridge ahead, go half-LEFT to a hidden ladder stile in the tree-clad ridge. Continue ahead to cross another low ridge and on through a wide gap in the trees. Descend to enter and cross a large field to a road. Follow it LEFT into Llandegla.

D rovers used to leave their animals near the old bridge over the river. Close to the village lies St Tegla's Holy Well, reputed to be the oldest healing well in Wales, famous for the cure of epilepsy until the early 19thC. Nearby is a large piece of sandstone, known locally as the 'Roman Stone', of great antiquity and possibly the missing village cross.

PRONUNCIATION

These basic points should help non-Welsh speakers

Welsh	English equivalent
c	always hard, as in cat
ch	as on the Scottish word lo**ch**
dd	as th in **then**
f	as f in of
ff	as ff in off
g	always hard as in got
ll	no real equivalent. It is like 'th' in **then**, but with an 'L' sound added to it, giving '**thlan**' for the pronunciation of the Welsh 'Llan'.

In Welsh the accent usually falls on the last-but-one syllable of a word.

KEY TO THE MAPS

- ➡ Walk route and direction
- ══ Metalled road
- ‒‒‒ Unsurfaced road
- •••• Footpath/route adjoining walk route
- ■□■ Railway
- ~~⤳ River/stream & flow
- ♣ ۞ Trees
- **G** Gate
- **S** Stile
- F.B. Footbridge
- ⊻ Viewpoint
- ℗ Parking
- ⊤ Telephone

THE COUNTRY CODE

- Be safe – plan ahead and follow any signs
- Leave gates and property as you find them
- Protect plants and animals, and take your litter home
- Keep dogs under close control
- Consider other people

The CroW Act 2000, implemented throughout Wales in May 2005, introduced new legal rights of access for walkers to designated open country, predominantly mountain, moor, heath or down, plus all registered common land. This access can be subject to restrictions and closure for land management or safety reasons for up to 28 days a year. The following web site operated by Countryside Council for Wales will provide updated information on any closures.
www.ccw.gov.uk

Useful telephone numbers:
Denbighshire Countryside Services   01352 810614
Denbighshire Highways Department   01824 706872
Flintshire Highways   01352 701233/4 for maintenance problems, and
01352 704612/3/9 for other queries.

Published by
Kittiwake 3 Glantwymyn Village Workshops, Glantwymyn, Machynlleth, Montgomeryshire SY20 8LY
© *Text & maps*: David Berry 2006
© *Illustrations*: Kittiwake 2006
Cover photographs by David Berry
Illustrations: Morag Perrott

Care has been taken to be accurate. However neither the author nor the publisher can accept responsibility for any errors which may appear, or their consequences. If you are in doubt about any access, check before you proceed.
Printed by MWL, Pontypool.
First edition 1999. Revised 2000/2003.
New revised and extended edition 2006, reprint 2007, 2008, 2009.
ISBN: **978 1 902302 42 3**